Relationships and Respon[sibilities] With Your Family

by Janet Gurtler

Butter Tarts

Butter Tarts is published by Beech Street Books
27 Stewart Rd. Collingwood, ON Canada L9Y 4M7

www.beechstreetbooks.ca

Produced by Red Line Editorial.

Photographs ©: andresr/iStockphoto, cover, 1; Fat Camera/iStockphoto, 5, 9; alvarez/iStockphoto, 6; Creatista/iStockphoto, 10; fstop123/iStockphoto, 13; monkeybusinessimages/iStockphoto, 15; vkyryl/iStockphoto, 17; shironosov/iStockphoto, 19; PeopleImages/iStockphoto, 20

Editor: Claire Mathiowetz
Designer: Laura Polzin

Library and Archives Canada Cataloguing in Publication

Gurtler, Janet, author
    With your family / by Janet Gurtler.

(Relationships and responsibilities)
Includes bibliographical references and index.
Issued in print and electronic formats.
ISBN 978-1-77308-136-6 (hardcover).--ISBN 978-1-77308-196-0 (softcover).--
ISBN 978-1-77308-256-1 (PDF).--ISBN 978-1-77308-295-0 (HTML)

    1. Families--Juvenile literature. I. Title.

HQ744.G87 2017   j306.85   C2017-903876-1
                                                 C2017-903877-X

Printed in the United States of America
Mankato, MN
August 2017

Table of Contents

Chapter 1

What Is a Family?

Families come in all shapes and sizes. Some children have two parents in the same house. Some families have parents and children living in different houses. Other children live with grandparents, foster parents, or **guardians**. It doesn't matter what someone's family looks like. The differences are what make each family special.

Every family is different, but all families are special!

5

Families are meant to care for each other. Family members should **respect** family rules. Children learn the rules in their families as they grow up. A child may have five **siblings** and live on a farm. Sometimes a child doesn't have siblings and lives in an apartment.

Each family has its own special traditions, such as cooking together.

Every family has its own **traditions**. Some traditions come from religious beliefs or cultural backgrounds. Many beliefs are passed down from **generations**.

Fun Fact

A family tradition can be a daily thing, such as always eating dinner at six o'clock. It can also be life-long, such as the way a family celebrates birthdays. Family traditions strengthen a sense of belonging and create memories.

Family History

Children are all part of a larger family group. In some families, children may not know all of their **relatives**. But everyone is an important part of their family's story.

Each child has **biological** parents. The parents of a child also have parents. These are a child's grandparents. Grandparents

Families can be made up of many different kinds of people.

also have parents, who are a child's great-grandparents. Families are much bigger than they appear.

Parents can be two dads, two moms, a single parent, or a dad and a mom. Some children are **adopted**. The people who adopt them are their parents. These children might have relationships with their biological parents, too. There are many ways to be a family.

There are other kinds of relatives, too. An extended family is someone's larger family outside the home. Often, extended family members are people such as

aunts or uncles. They are the brothers and sisters of the child's parents. But friends are sometimes considered family, too.

All families look different. Many children have sisters and brothers. Some children have half-sisters or half-brothers. This means that a sibling has one of the same parents, but not both. There are stepsisters or stepbrothers, too. These are siblings who live together in a **blended family**.

Many extended families get together for special occasions, such as holidays and birthdays.

3

The Role of Parents or Guardians

Families should look after each other. Parents or guardians are usually the leaders of families. They are responsible for children's basic needs. These are things that everyone needs to survive. Basic needs are food, warmth, shelter, and clothing.

Parents or guardians should make sure kids have healthy food to eat. Sometimes kids can even help pick out the food!

Families should make sure children have enough food to eat. Shelter means that families live in a safe home. This could be a house, apartment, condo, or townhouse. This home gives children a place to sleep and live comfortably.

Parents and guardians are there to love and care for their children. They should set examples of good behaviour and what is right and wrong. Parents and guardians should listen to children talk about their problems and their dreams.

Parents and guardians must make sure their children go to school. They can help children find their place in the world. Children need to learn how to be good citizens. Parents and guardians can help them do that.

Home can mean something different to everyone. Not everyone lives in the same kind of house!

Chapter

4

The Role of a Child

Children play an important **role** in their families. It's great for kids to talk about their day with their parents or guardians. It keeps families close. Children learn about life and form **values** from their families.

Families teach children how to get along with others. Parents and guardians set up

One way kids can help around the house is by washing dishes.

rules to make sure children learn and grow well. Children should help around the family home. They may have chores to do. Some chores are clearing the table or taking out the garbage. Chores teach kids new skills.

Families should make sure children are looked after. Kids need to go to

Another role kids can have in the family is to help take care of any pets. They can do this by walking, washing, or feeding the pet.

bed at set times to make sure they get enough sleep. They also need to eat a **balanced** diet to stay healthy. Children need time to play and do

Fun Fact
How much money do you think it costs to raise a child in a family? In 2017, the average cost of raising a child from birth until 18 years of age in Canada was almost $250,000!

things they enjoy, but they also have to help. Responsibilities teach kids how to function in our world. Families teach kids many things they need to know to grow up properly.

Glossary

adopted

legally taken as the child of a non-biological parent

balanced

appropriate in content and amounts

blended family

a family made up of children or parents from more than one family

generations

groups of people born in a certain time frame

guardians

someone who watches over a child but might not be related to that child

relatives

people who are part of someone's family

respect

polite and considerate

role

a part that someone plays

siblings

sisters or brothers

traditions

beliefs or customs that are handed down over time

values

beliefs that are important to people, such as honesty

To Learn More

Books

Geisen, Cynthia. *Growing Into a Family: A Kid's Guide to Living in a Blended Family*. St. Meinrad, IN: Abbey Press, 2015.

Simon, Norma. *All Kinds of Families*. Park Ridge, IL: Albert Whitman & Company, 2016.

Waddell, Dan. *Who Do You Think You Are? Be a Family Tree Detective*. Somerville, MA: Candlewick Press, 2011.

Websites

All Kids Network: Family
https://www.allkidsnetwork.com/worksheets/family/

Child and Youth Health: Families
http://www.cyh.com/HealthTopics/HealthTopicDetailsKids.aspx?p=335&np=282&id=1524

PBS Kids: Family
http://pbskids.org/itsmylife/family/index.html

Index

Quick Questions

- What rules does your family have at mealtime? Why do you have those rules?

- Describe the people in your family home. What is your role in your family? What are things you do to help out?

- Think about a tradition your family has. Do you have a certain meal on a certain day?

- Does your family always do an activity together? How do you celebrate birthdays? Describe one of your family traditions.